Sky's Lines

Odes to

The Ether

D. Ellsworth Hoag

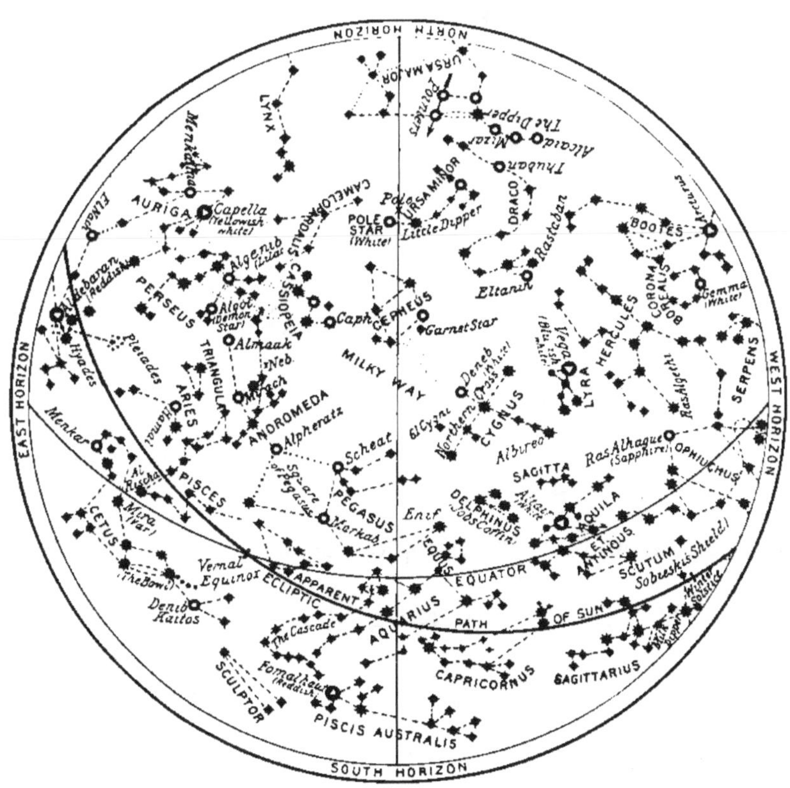

Graphics from publicdomainpictures.net

LIBRA
VIRGO
LEO
CANCER
GEMINI
TAURUS
ARIES
PISCES
AQUARIUS
CAPRICORNUS
SAGITTARIUS
SCORPIO
A
B
C
D
E
F
G
H
R

Enigma

Cubic miles of heavy air
tinted to a light cyan,
charcoal in the depths of night—
enigma for man.

We observe flaring sunspots,
correlate them to events;
play dot to dot with the stars
in the firmament.

We track moon's changing phases
notice how she pulls the tide
so we can catch the apex—
safe from harbor glide.

We see sunrise and sunset
walk across horizon’s rim
marking celestial seasons
a slow stately hymn.

As early as the druids
with mysticism and fear
man would plan festivals by
the wheel of the year.

And so we see that skylines
are not just where earth meets sky
they’re celestial theorems
on what phases imply.

Then, if you add poetry,
sky lines go on forever,
for mystery and folklore
wonder deliver.

Contents

Early Stroll

When

dawn,

crimson

and scarlet

is painted ‘cross the sky—

sun’s orb still ‘neath the horizon,

and night is ‘bout to die

no shadows

are cast

on

earth.

A walk

beside a dog

to watch dark turn to light,

it is a most pleasant ending

to night.

Early Meditation

The morrowdim glows faintly
and the world's still soft and dim
as the sun awakens nature
by kissing horizon's rim.

Like an old married couple
they slow-creep into the day
and the sky blushes scarlet
as it watches their foreplay.

There are not any shadows
for the light is still diffuse—
it seems to break the silence
tis a terrible abuse.

And thus we wait in limbo

‘til the sun mounts to the sky

and finally stop our reverie

when long shadows meet the eye.

Sunset Drive

Light blue and peach pink

The sky loitering at night's brink

A quiet time of reverie

On desert, mountain, plain, sea.

On a short trip, just me,

I would like to drive to eternity.

This is the feeling of free

Nothing to prove, just to be.

So when saffron light's on the lea

Leave me be with my dreams and tea.

Visual Textures

Herringbone clouds—watery night sky,
misty moon glances through ripples.
'Tis a night where dragons might fly
and startle the world with their cry.
Welkin folds like wind-sculptured sand,
soft paper-lantern light infused,
a sky from an artisan's hand—
the ceiling of a wonder land.
The cool desert air holds the night
and vision is not crystal clear;
for distance seems ever so slight
could caress heavens in delight.
Inspiration oft is a hint,
but this time, it is evident.

Ode to Pillars of Day (2)

oh scarlet sunrise

doorway to another day

I praise your promise

oh saffron sunset

silent sentinel of sweet night

whose rest I require

gateposts and pillars

that support and separate time

supreme, yet simple

our souls rest in surety

'cause your currents are constant

Any Time Is Show Time

The sky

puts on a show—

it's only for my eye

fluffy folk and monsters pass by

a parade of wispy white 'gainst the blue

some bring a giggle some a sigh,

but I will share with you

tickets are free—

attend.

Ode to The Pillars of Day

The plains of heaven are on fire
as Helios banks the dying blaze
the flames lick the low cloud edges
and heaven emits a rose haze.

He puts his feet on the fender
and readies for night tide repose.
Slowly the embers fade to black
as he deeper into slumber goes.

But at appointed time to rise
he urges the hot ash to flame
hitches his steeds to chariot
and hastens dark skies to reclaim.

Thus morn and eve are halcyon

with the warmness of firelight glow

a time when wayward reveries

arrive once more to peace bestow.

Twilight

I went out walking with my dog,
the sun was getting low,
and all the scene about me
infused with rosy glow.

Western sky was turning saffron,
gold-gilted clouds flow,
and I knew that I was walking
into crepusculo.

As I continued on my way
I felt a bit slow
arthritis in my hip and back
were staging a show.

And though I briskly strode along

I truly did know

each step on my earthly path led

into crepusculo.

But I have found rewards in life,

so though day is low

I discovered a contentment

in crepusculo.

Winter Walk

In the south, popcorn clouds dappled with patches of blue
resolving to liquid azure at heaven's azimuth
then developing into layers of slate in the north.

The light was muted winter-bright, a shadow glare,
the distance from the sun gave it an aqueous aura
an illumination befitting for artistic half-tones.

The mid-morning air was coffee lightly creamed,
brisk but with the edge taken off,
tasting of slightly warmed desert soil.

The poodle by my side was light buff with some tan
and had the texture of fine velvet
a large canine, but gentle and full of love.

A slight burning in my thighs from walking,

a smile upon my face from excellent companionship.

The ambience of contentment bordering on perfection.

Sonoran Summer Sky

The

sky

o'erhead

a blue bowl

empty, but for light.

Evenly colored it stretches

forth glorious and pristine to touch the horizon.

Cool blue it starts the morning trek,

but burns to blue white,

bleached in the

sun's heat

by

noon.

Then

late

evening

adds more dye

'til azure again.

Then of a sudden sun does drop

and blue fades slowly to the ebony of darkness.

Night bounded by red horizon

returns one more time

then cedes to

blue bowl

o'er

earth.

Night Tide

You can hear the loon
sing a plaintive tune
as he begins to fly.

The full-faced moon
is a silver rune
hung in a purple sky.

Ebony tree pillars, lattice- capped
guard the night while mortals nap
as stars twinkle nigh.

On hollow tree woodpecker taps
and night-time owl softly flaps
hunting on the fly.

Soaring spires stand proud and tall,
flying buttresses, nature's cathedral,
pines piercing the sky.

Answering the moon's call
seas rise from their fall
staining at earth's tie.

Northwest Winter

You look out your window

and see the rain;

you look out your window

again and again.

You look out your window

at a flannel grey sky

and pray that spring

will soon come by.

Night Rain

The moon had lost its splendor;
the stars were blotted out;
stark silence filled the nighttime,
nature held its breath in doubt.

The air trembled with tension;
all was shrouded by the dark
'til Zeus in sudden anger
threw forth his heavenly spark.

Then leaden skies erupted
and the universe did cry.
The earth was truly bathed,
'twas no longer sere and dry.

Reason for Jubilation

When the moon has lost her luster
and the stars have almost fled,
between three and four in the morning,
is the hour of the dead.

This is the darkest part of the night
for human folk to dread
for this is the hour that marks
the floodtide of souls fled.

So say a little blessing
before you go abed
and sing *Hallelujah*
when you waken not dead.

Ode to Summer Morn

Dawn is on the horizon,
glowing, pink, and new;
the lark is in the clear air;
the grass bejeweled with dew.

Sun rays paint long shadows,
the world in bas relief.
It all seems so perfect
that we stare in disbelief.

Morning, summer breeze,
warm and rich like toast,
enjoy it while you may,
by noon you'll likely roast.

Eternity Myth

In the darkest part of the night
when the moon and stars don't shine
and the world seems abandoned
by the light-hearted and divine.

When no forgiving finger
reaches down from cloven skies
and the scene is all the same
through closed or open eyes.

Then we feel at the whim of fate,
a disorienting sensation,
'til we feel our souls scourged
by ambivalent vilification.

For the Fates in a square dance
form a circle then a star;
come close to embrace you
and then ignore you from afar.

But it all is just a dream,
or at least so some folks say,
for the feeling often goes away
with the dawning of the day.

Thus you must make your mind up;
build your own eternity myth.
Then change it any time you like
until you reach your death.

Pre Precipitation

The sky is gray

a dismal day

will it be rain or snow

how do we know.

It’s in the shade

the sky has made

we may come to foretell

by learning well.

Observe the tint

there lies the hint

experience will show

then may we know.

I saw snow gray

in the desert

and learned that tinted glass

truth can pervert.

Lines on Sky

We arise in the morning
and observe the arc of sky
a portent of the coming day
we wish to imply.

Some days the sky is mellow,
sometimes it's primary bright.
On occasion scant white clouds,
or flotillas white.

We learn that heaven's fickle,
sometimes will disclose the day,
but may play close to the vest,
then give what it may.

Enjoy the day come what may,
skylines should stay a poet's lay.

Thunder Storm

Clouds, cannonball stacks in the sky,
threaten that heaven's peace will die.
Lightning muzzle-flashes then fly
and thunderous volleys do reply.
We know the war is drawing nigh
and pray destruction pass us by,
for sometimes striking from on high
a charge will reach the earth nearby.
Yet, we our fears would fain deny and wait
'til fate clears all—post heaven's cry.

Eclipse

The moon rose faint pale
in the early evening sky
wearing a wispy cloud veil,
faintly hidden from the eye.

The darkness only a trace
and the night just at birth,
I didn't see her cover her face
with the shadow of the earth.

When night at last was present
the moon had slipped the cloud
But her light was already spent,
she had her shadow shroud.

She hung like a paper lantern
on the eastern edge of sky;
Parchment brown was her skin
tinged red like fire was nigh.

She looked far in the distance,
yet was such a perfect sphere
So vivid was her countenance
I felt like ‘twas done with mirrors.

For about an hour and thirty
that she kept this darkened hue
And though somehow pretty,
my impatience quickly grew.

Then there came a touch of silver
like a well-shined Sunday spoon
That made a bright white sliver
on the top-left of the moon.

Along the line earth's shadow
made her border appear to grow,
small looked the part in the shade,
large the bright side seemed to glow.

Twenty minutes earth’s round shadow
slid across the moon’s dark trace
and with awe my voice said, "Ohhh",
as she revealed her shiny face.

So always I see the firmament
where the stars and planets spin—
man is so small and insignificant
we must find ourselves again.

Rainbow 1

A

pale

rainbow

in the sky

the soft glow of love

simple and unornamented.

It is redolent—

of mother's

gentle,

soft

touch.

Waxing Gibbous

The

moon's

waxing

now gibbous

hanging like tilted

silver goblet in the night sky

stem and base enveloped in a divinity's hand

ambrosia trickles to the earth

inebriating

with a soft

calming

pale

light.

Faint

webbed

halo

is magic

seeping through the glass

the gods baptize our Mother Earth

poor mortals view this outpouring with unstinted awe

like a priest blessing eucharist,

thin white sacred disc,

wine—partake—

body

and

blood

Aurora Borealis

In

the

cold north

it begins,

tiny particles

emitted from the sun's surface

transfer their small charge

as they hit

the earth's

thick

air.

There

they

excite

the atoms

in the atmosphere

and make nature’s own neon lights.

which glow green and pink.

In the dark

of night.

they

shine.

Then

do

dances

and ripple,

slow, and sensual,

A green and pink curtain it flows,

this heavenly art

of the north

painting

cold

air.

Rainbow 2

rainbows

skittles of light

misty and transcendent

a flavor ravished by the eye

rainbows

Tornado

The air moves in giant circles
twists of clouds like dirty, grey licorice whips

Tree limbs,
boards ripped from houses,
miscellany
appear and vanish, rise and fall.

Ma Nature's temper tantrum
roils
as air itself becomes weapon of choice.
When storm passes
it leaves the earth a disheveled bed
cluttered, filled with offal—silent, alone, and sad

Watercolor

Rainbows are water colors,
you know they are,
they're soft and misty
and best viewed from afar.

A sign that Mother Nature
is changing her mind.
Means "I've been nasty,
but now shall be kind. "

Benefit of Age

Like children we lay in the grass,
our faces caressed by the sun,
in wonder gazing at the clouds
seeing fairy tales one by one.

We see myriad of shapes,
animals scuttle ‘cross the blue,
and our minds revert to childhood
as years melt like morning dew.

Reaching out to little teachers,
young children who recline nearby,
spirit-guides who lead us to truths
that are secreted in the sky.

Do not wonder why grandparents
have a smile and a twinkling eye
for they learned to play once again
as if the years stopped passing by.

Love and Hope

The beauty didn't strike me,

even though I looked.

The moon was a silver button

on the blue greatcoat of God,

the stars the embroidery

adorning His matching vest.

A loved one's death had fallen on me,

an axe to the headsman's block.

It was balm when my lover said,

"I will follow you into the darkness."

But love lessened the blackness to
morrowdim all around.
I knew dawn was coming and
the lark again would sound,
that life would have its rhythm
and reason have its rhyme
then I'd step from grief's dark tunnel
into a brighter time.

Sylvan Skyline

Trees against the sky
a moving lacework of green
translucent in spring.

The leaves in summer
solid with mere peeks of sky
dappling the light.

Fall's kaleidoscope
bright colors flash against blue
dancing in the wind.

Bare twigs of winter
rattle 'neath wintry sky
dueling spider webs.

Cold color of winter sky

fini of a passing year.

Messages

Some say the Fates are stellar,
that they write upon the stars
and within their sacred words
are triumphs and scars.

Some feel rotating planets
the auspicious times relate
thus the movement of their dance
shows the proper date.

A search for hidden meaning
draws a zodiac in the sky
which mystics read for portents
using their third eye

Thus sky becomes a mystic
who converses with men’s souls
and connects them to unknowns
as it features scroll.

Dawn

Pouring from the sun's pitcher
light spills o'er horizon rim.
The edge of day approaches
in a glow both soft and dim.

Then the brilliant dawn splashes
across the eastern fringe of sky,
in a multi-hued cocktail
to intoxicate the eye.

If you want ambrosia
you don’t even need a cup,
simply open up your soul
and joyfully drink it up.

Yearning

Thin white lines

cross the sky

stretch in front.

Make me think

of far off

sights I love.

Oh, contrails

you speak of

adventure.

Infinity

Sky, symbol of infinity,
spawning place of divinity,
built to produce an awe-filled pause,
to question man's natural laws,
cause search for true serenity.

Thus we will have affinity
for this blue vicinity
as men must hide religion's flaws
in symbol of infinity.

Like oceans of salinity

doubts can etch our serenity

until we're in conundrum's jaws

and inner demons' frightful caws

drive us to sky's vicinity,

symbol of infinity.

How Day Should be Bookended

The dawn should be a fanfare,
a morning's clarion call
with red and gold that echoes
off of every pool and wall.

A joyous invitation
to the festival of day
so with anticipation
we proceed upon our way.

To waken us with brilliance
both of color and of light
inspire us with boldness
so we meet our tasks with might.

But sunset should be mellow.
tinted pink, saffron, and cream
to lull us toward slumber,
lead to soft and gentle dream.

Diffuse glow without dazzle
to rest daytime-weary eye
so all distress and anger
are let out with one long sigh.

Of Two Minds

Cloud cover
mediates
temperature.

In winter
holds the heat
down to earth.

In summer
holds the heat
o’er the world.

Sky Map

The stars cast in space's vastness,
organized by seafaring men,
become a celestial roadmap
of vast spaces without byways.
For constellations are devised
which walk the heavens as earth moves.
Thus math and measurement can tell
your place on terrestrial plane.
The important skylines are found
by careful sextant measurements.
This aids the roaming ways of man
and helps him reach his final goal.
Thus star charts known as sky maps give
credence to lost on cloudy night.

Now Wait

Clustered at sky's edge
striated flint-colored clouds
look gravid with rain

They march in dark ranks
quarter way to sky's apex
glower at the earth

not dark with thunder
but somber and determined
they promise of rain

not yet the ozone
just a forecast in heavens
that may be fulfilled

sky of anticipation

sign to prepare the rain gear.

Wind of Déja vu

The cliff

sloped steep downward

to meet the open sea

the updraft on my face brings

recall.

Recall

of a large kite

tugged upward to the sky

its shape against the blue etched on

my eye.

My eye

views once again

a bright tropical sky,

soft breezes waft remembrance

to me

To me,

a younger man

who stands beside his bride,

the years just seem to drift away

and hide.

And hide

in bright, clear sky,

to drift with fluffy clouds

across the azure, welkin dome—

goodbye.

Full of Hot Air

many large baskets
bright fabric sacks lay in field
roar of propane fires

sacks morph into orbs
ropes strain against holding spikes
chaos of voices

tethers soon are loosed
slow graceful rise of balloons
sigh chorus of awe

the thrill is still there
a spectacle old, yet new
glorious to view

the kaleidoscopic hues

Christmas bulbs against blue sky

Illusion

On a calm sea

'neath a clear sky

horizon disappears.

Where blue meets blue

it seems the two

converge and simply merge.

A hemisphere

it does appear

ocean base—heaven's curve.

Deity's hand

a trick has planned,

made skyline disappear.

Sky Secrets

For millennia man scanned the skies
seeking answers in stars' bright eyes,
but the universe rebuked
and hid its secrets well
for Fates have decreed
they shan't succeed
for there is
always
more.

A Pastel

A coral reef-like ring surrounds
a gem-like sea of clearest blue;
sunset glows the whole horizon,
heaven’s bowl rimmed in a soft hue.

As seeing rainbow from above,
the rays have scribed a circle light,
giving for some fleeting moments
a halo round welkin ere night

And as I watch the colors fade
I know the night time soon will spread
a velvet scarf embossed with stars
to cover her beauteous head.

Somehow I feel tranquility

that this is painted for my soul

and nature often gives to man

pastel pictures to make them whole.

Contrast

The skyline made by man
is angular or square—
just touched on occasion
with an arc here or there.

But, nature's are free-form
her skylines won't conform
you think you've seen it all
then find there is no norm.

So fix your eyes where earth meets skies
and visualize infinity.

Lost

On

a cloudy night

the sky

disappears.

The heavenly lights are

smothered by a gray, wool blanket.

Our guideposts are obliterated

and somehow we are even more alone,

for all is black on ebon.

We take comfort in skylines that once were.

Sky Watch

The sun, the moon, and the stars—
the universe's timepiece
that first showed man time's passage
as they coursed the sky.

They tell many useful things;
when to wake and when to sleep,
when to plant, when harvest,
they're heavenly seers.

Thus time is ever tied to
the solar systems movement
as it spirals on through space—
yes, symbiotic.

And thus it is no wonder

gods abide in the heavens

it seems only just and right

since power bides there.

The Why of The Sky

It's said

the atmosphere

scatters the sun's fair light

and what reflects to earth is blue,

the sky.

The sky,

dawn and sunset

paints it in tones near red

for rays pass through more of earth's air

disperse.

Disperse

these varied hues,

a splendor to the eye,

to announce the bookends of day

for us.

For us—

and our children

ask why the sky is blue

and we tell them quite sincerely,

"Just because."

Two Faces

When Diana walks the daytime sky

her countenance is wan and pale

she seems almost transparent

and wondrously frail

near the horizon

she seems to float

on sky sea—

lunar

boat.

But

when she

comes at night

her face is bright

and she fills the scene

with transcendent white light.

To show us her preference—

during the day listless she'll roam

at night a regal queen on her throne.

Blue to Blue

In

the

Blue Ridge

Mountain Range,

grazing from the crest,

blue undulates in frozen waves,

meets with the sky at

horizon—

a line

scant

seen.

And

yet

where the

waves cease is

a blurred divide,

for in that world of misty blue

the globe edge blends with

welkin hue

defies

a

line.

And

on

some days

heavens seem

to fall in ripples

and lay upon earth's ample breast

and then it appears

one can climb

foothills

to

sky.

A Soft Touch

Clouds are stroked on the heavens,
dry-brushed to be feathery,
swept up like painted eyebrows
on a cool blue face.
And sky's cosmetologist
slowly sweeps some powder puffs
betwixt—caressing clear skin,
enhancing beauty.
And these few final touches
that frame her fair countenance
somehow give soft expression
to a plain, bright face.
It becomes a gentle sky
which asks all to come and play.

Early Darkness

The daylight dims to twilight gray
although not half-way through the day ——
thick clouds impasto on the sky,
both dark and fearsome to the eye,
morph to thunderheads on display

Static builds in clouds' disarray
and lightning strobes begin to play—
spring into sight and quick do die—
twilight grey.

Thunder rolls down sky's blackened ways,

loud evidence of nature's sway,

and then the welkin starts to cry,

torrential downpour streaming by.

Until the rain does pass away—

twilight grey.

Define

Skylines,

heaven meets earth,

blue backdrop to landscape—

but to poet it's lines of verse,

skylines.

Which is

more beautiful?

One appeals to the eye,

one touches the ear and the heart—

which is?

Blue void

accepts your awe,

however it is shown,

repays with bright sun and night's jewels—

Blue void.

Sky's Circle of Life

Red stained horizon;

Day bleeds out so Night may reign.

Crepusculo falls,

sun now past the horizon,

faint twilight glow hangs o'er all.

Light fades down to black

as moon slowly scales the sky.

Ebon lid of night

births multitudinous stars,

adds glows to the firmament.

At fullness of dark

Nature pronounces Day dead.

Night now in full reign.

Nocturnal law does decree

Night will die when comes the dawn.

Picture Show

The heavens are an etch-a-sketch
when white clouds decorate the sky
and morph to different images
as they drift slowly by.

For in the welkin blows the wind
which reshapes fluffy white masses
and innocents watch in amaze
as the parade passes.

And with warm sunlight on the face
even the old can come to know
the joy of childlike wonderment
as visions come and go.

Depth Perception

The air is dry, the sun is bright,
the firmament is full of light,
and white clouds billow through the height.
The view is a 3D delight—
clear, crisp images greet our sight.
A stately movement to their flight,
they pass dressed in angelic white.
Their movement's surreal, never trite.
Layer on layer they incite the soul
to extol heaven's depth and might.

Arizona Thought

A grey woolen glove,

the sky close and intimate;

light soft and diffuse.

Now in solitude,

wrapped in a soft grey swaddle,

there's a sense of peace

A winter skyscape

matte and drab becomes earth's lid

no demarcations.

Duskiness meets white,

invokes muted sight and sound,

scene in solemn tones.

Seattle snowtime flashback,

nostalgia without remorse.

Lake View

The lake, a mirror on a calm day,

causes horizon's disarray

for who can say what is sky.

The clouds that float in heavens blue

swim in the water's surface too—

fair twins to observer's eye.

Blue Sky

Sky

is blue,

that is true,

or so it's said.

Howe'er I would eschew—

never be too docilely led.

Some things once said simply live in the head

If we accept without thinking at all—oh my!

I viewed for years and most ardently read

thick tomes many people would dread

and I found many hue

both gray and red

'tis not true

just—blue

sky.

Indecisive Rainbags

Scientists give clouds a name

but all the same the meaning

doesn’t always seem to fit—

clouds’re set on inbetweening.

False Night

A sandstorm nears,

horizon lifts.

Sand rises up high

embraces sky.

Faux horizon

breeds a known fear—

surreal night's nigh.

Scrim

God was feeling bad ‘bout his plan
creation was good, then came man.
He thought about the glut of sin
its miasma might do him in.

Thought that a blue inverted bowl
might shelter Him from tainted souls.
He’d fix it up with trinkets bright
to distract man by day or night.

He would put holes in this great lid
so all his creatures won’t be dead.
Humans would call each hole a star
to guide them from heaven afar.

He could obscure with many clouds
when the cacophony was too loud.
And He could still watch with delight
when everything was going right.

Ah yes, the sky is just a scrim
employed by the almighty Him.

Sun Break

The sun shines through the cloud cover,
a worn spot on a ragged suit.
Brings hope things will improve anon
and brightens tedium's gloom.

Oh, pray o'ercast will burn off soon—
the sun shines through the cloud cover.
Now shinier the thinned site grows,
and stirs excitement in the soul.

A spotlight of sunlight breaks through,
paints a small patch of bright color.
The sun shines through the cloud cover,
now hope becomes reality.

How like to life a cloudy day,

reminding us bad things will pass—

joy will be painted on the soul—

the sun shines through the cloud cover.

Holiday Sky

The evening sky glowed
a red, that was close to orange—
ambience of fall.

Ebon silhouettes
etched sharp on the horizon.
Halloween sunset.

Should beckon a moon
round, bright and red in the east
looming large and lucent.

Surreal skyline
hovers in winter welkin—
beauty and disquiet.

Unrest fades as does the light—

there is solace in the night.

Limits

The sky
is the limit,
thus people will decry,
the price has gone sky high—
the sky.

The sky
is the daydream,
there is pie in the sky
and each day will be a feast day—
the sky.

The sky
it is falling
Chicken Little declares,
so the ultimate doom also—
the sky.

The sky

will never fall

but it will crack withal

and the earth will warm and die sans

the sky.

The sky

must continue

else all good things will cease

thus we must constantly protect—

the sky.

Bird Flight

How does the little bird-a-roo

soar through the heavens wide and blue?

He does an aerobatic fly

with mighty pinions on each wing

and rudders on his backside thing—

he dances through the azure sky.

Love's Lament

Lunar rise over sifting dunes,
white sand waves 'neath a silver rune,
reminds me of a jazz harp tune.
The hollow sounds like a lone loon
makes one long for fair afternoon.
Then in between sand does croon,
"Alas my love departs too soon.
Oh, grant to me a single boon.
Let my sweetheart a moment swoon o'er me—
then she with love her heart festoon.

Air Show

Starlings by the hundreds wheel across the sky.

They pivot,

in a moment

invert their flying formation.

ar, then in a split second d
o i
They s v
e.

Unpredictable ballet of black on blue.

S
p
i
r
a
l
s that overlap,
flowing in sensuous curves,

moving through quadrants.

Graceful as a ballet,

precise as a drill team.

Divine op-art.

Fine New Day

New day
at morrowdim,
sun below the earth's rim
and red just starts on eastern sky,
new day.

New day,
stark silhouettes
against still darkened blue,
earth still awaits its daytime hue
new day.

New day,
the sky brightens
rose and cream climbs heaven
and earth soon will be given
new day.

New day,

a scarlet disc

arrives on the skyline

and promises truly fine

new day.

Raining Tears

Pacific Northwest skies weep,

a soft and sustained drizzle.

In the Southwest, heavens cry,

large-drop, splashing downpour.

It makes me think of grieving,

gentle grief that tends to last;

wailing and gnashing of teeth

is too hard to sustain.

Does nature call for volume?

Is grief measured in inches?

When tears do not fall heavy,

does the grieving prolong?

Tears lave the pain from the soul—

the water that makes us whole.

Gray Flannel

Mundane sky

blasé gray

uninspired.

Not brilliant,

nor even

lowering.

No promise

except for

soft lighting.

Surreal Sky

A

Phoenix

afternoon,

cumulus clouds

march across the heavens,

etched in relief by hidden sun.

Sharp outlined mounds like white meringue

the bases flat—enrobed in dove gray garb.

Horizon wears stratocumulus mass that breaks

into individual popcorn puffs.

Polarized sunglass-surreal,

no glare to mute each edge,

color strangely strong,

not found in

nature.

Man

made.

As One

Mare tail clouds scroll cross the sky
white wood-grain on azure hue.
Russet roof-tiles, mesquite, palm
etch themselves ‘gainst blue.

Phoenix skyline from close view;
day’s bright orb dangles at ten.
In The Valley Of The Sun
springtime heat begins.

Sitting there looking southward
warm contentment fills my soul
and I feel I am conjoined
with the cosmic whole.

Succor

Mammatus clouds in dark sky,

globular masses below cloud base,

Ma Nature's popcorn ceiling.

The sky looks like bubble wrap,

mayhaps a reminder to mankind,

earth though hearty—still fragile.

Heaven's mammary glands,

a promise for succor in our need

if we treat her with respect.

Arrival

The skyline of home is delight,
viewed by either day or by night,
redolent of family and friends,
it's harbinger of travail's end—
rest from the world's turmoil and fright.

Yes, any time we see that sight
each tension eases—all is aright
as every worry starts to mend—
the skyline of home.

If topping crest or ending flight,
when well known silhouettes bedight
the edge of sky's lucent, blue bend,
we know our journey's near its end
thus we await with all our might—
the skyline of home.

Dutch Fashion

"'Tis a fortunate portend," folks say,

"Dutch pants worth of blue means a nice day."

But in the heavens is mostly grey—

hope Holland trends skinny jeans today.

Early Spring Night

The moon was parchment yellow
slung low in the eastern sky.
The firmament had dim light
though night lingered nigh.

Diana was out walking
her entourage was not near.
Somehow ‘twas melancholy—
blues in heaven clear.

Lonesome, sad harmonica
seemed redolent of the scene
for somehow those hollow tones
made it seem more serene.

Sometimes Mother Nature writes
background for a tune.

Conundrum

Naught—of blue,

hue of air,

name of sky.

Translucent,

non-opaque,

special dye.

Ah, physics

you confound

human eye.

Gradients

You hear anguish, angst, and pain
when first listening to the blues,
but soon you get the message
it has various hues.

When viewing the arching sky
it at first seems even blue,
but when watching with keen eye
it has various hues.

In springtime ‘tis robin egg,
in summer ‘tis bleached with light,
in fall ‘tis soft and mellow,
winter cold and bright.

But yet more astonishing,
is the gradient of blue
that fills a bright and cloudless sky—
noted by some few.

The quadrant where the sun rides
seems to have a wash of white
while the regions farther off
are more tinted and bright.

So nothing is just simple
and naught is completely true
for even in reasoning
there is many a hue.

Dark Hour

Did a dragon eat the sun?
Did Helios turn his back?
Is he simply winking now;
is he coming back?

Twilight of solar eclipse
always brings back ancient fears
that old Sol has forsook us
after all these years.

And when his radiant face
finally harkens into view
our souls rejoice to the Fates
that ushered us through.

Dare to Play

In Phoenix saw a phoenix
hanging white ‘gainst blue sky
wings spreading long pinions,
a delight to watching eye.

A heavily plumed long tail
softly scrolling out behind
left a glorious image
etched upon my eager mind.

Some think that with aging
imagination fades away—
but the real truth is many
just won’t let it out to play.

From Cloven Skies

Sunburst,

clouds split in twain,

cumulus piles cloven,

and bright rays erupt o'er heaven.

Shafts spreading out in massive arcs,

a wondrous sight at any time of day,

but glorious in the golden glow of daybreak.

It does beget the halos of the saints,

gilts the stand for the Eucharist.

A badge of honor or

symbol of hope—

sunburst.

Sky Mirage

The

gods

overlay

heavens in

gradients of gray—

you might expect some rain today.

Mirage in the sky—

in deserts

clouds oft

do

lie.

When you

see the raindrops

that is the only proof

creosote then states, “It’s no spoof,

rainfall.”

Sepia

An atmospheric brown cloud,
pollution floating in air,
raising one point eight miles
from the earth's surface.

It scatters and absorbs light,
disturbing nature's pattern,
poisoning the ecosphere,
obscuring clear sight.

When temperature inversion
holds it to Mother Earth's breast
breathing becomes hazardous,
burn bans put in place.

A foul fog made by mankind

causing a gritty filter

obscuring—soft-focusing—

skyline, grime meets grime.

Pray some eternal power

helps humankind to perceive

this road leads to destruction—

and truly believe.

Celestial Surf

lines of frothy clouds,
surf in the heavens,
though they do not move
I hear ocean's roar.

the air taints with salt,
lines of frothy clouds—
seabirds mewl and cry
nostalgia now reigns

many years seaside
surge in desert heat—
lines of frothy clouds
bring back memories

the past never dies

it’s just tucked away

comfort from times past—

lines of frothy clouds

Celestial Surf 2

Lines of feathery clouds stretch tier upon tier. Like surf in the sky, wave after wave, a still life against the ocean blue where currents meet some hidden reef. In wonder I am transported.

midday reverie
ocean thought to desert brought
closing in on me

the crashing of waves
the seaside smells that sudden swells
my inner thoughts laves

then I awestruck list
to sea bird calls that soft falls
through the salt-wind mist

I walk sea-wet sand

and low-tide odors abide

foreign to this land

thus I create in my pate

from cloud design scenes divine

Primal Response

A penumbra on the moon,
first hint of waning.
Definition blurred on one edge,
night's light slowly draining..

Diana starts her menstruation,
the oceans note her flow.
Tides change to fit her condition
as crickets sing largo.

Slowly she is devoured
by the dragon of the sky
until fully ingested
as the days go by.

E'en modern man watching
feels a pang of grief
which defies science,
is nurtured by primal belief.

We fear she left us,
that finally she did die,
in unbidden anguish
we raise a mournful cry.

Magical thinking continues
as celestial rebirth comes
and our souls hear the beating
of the jungle drums.

Cosmic Cotillion

Planets and stars pirouette—spin around,
while music of the spheres beats on the ear;
the divine cranks a handle and the sound,
of hurdy-gurdy grinding does appear.
A dance to the same monotonous beat—
a pavane with slow, somber, stately step
until we tread the dance with weary feet
dragging our cares we ever onward schlep.
All becomes a recital of *ennuyeux*,
a round that repeats unchanged forever.

I'm Done

The

heavens

stretch above

wondrous to see

reaching infinity—

but poems can only say so much

and exploring can be a reach too far.

I'll attempt to be wise—stop ere interest demise.

If I rambled—prolonged this theme too far

may reader forgive faltering wit.

And now good night to sky,

a fond adieu.

Audience

farewell

to

you.

www.ingramcontent.com/pod-product-compliance
Lightning Source LLC
LaVergne TN
LVHW012116170826
845678LV00014BA/2961